T0011537

Little Sticker Dolly Dressing
Kittens

Written by Fiona Watt
Illustrated by Lizzie Mackay
Designed by Antonia Miller

Contents

A new kitten

Izzy and Nina are looking for a new kitten. They want
to choose one that isn't too shy and likes to play.
It's very hard to decide which one they like best.

Izzy

Nina

Visiting the vet

Lauren has brought her kitten Pepper to see the vet because he has hurt his paw. He'd been hiding in a big cardboard box and caught his leg as he jumped out.

Robyn

Lauren

In the garden

It's a sunny afternoon and the kittens are playing in the garden. They love to hide in flowerpots, and try to catch the butterflies that are fluttering around.

Millie

Emily

Cat café

Ruby loves kittens but she doesn't have one of her own, so she's visiting a special café where there are lots of kittens she can play with.

Ruby

Freya

10

Catching leaves

It's a blustery day and the wind is blowing leaves from the trees. The kittens are trying to catch the leaves as they tumble to the ground.

Lara

Lola

Maddie

Feeding time

Lola and Maddie are helping to feed the kittens at
a rescue shelter for stray cats and kittens. They hope
all the kittens will find new homes very soon.

A play date

Most kittens love playing together. Jessie and Mia have brought their kittens to Alice's house so that all the kittens can play games and have lots of cuddles.

Jessie

Alice

Mia

Orla

Pet store

Orla's looking for a new toy for her kitten, Muffin. She's chosen a little toy mouse that Muffin can hunt and pounce on.

Emma

17

Cassie

Exploring outside

Cassie and Leah love watching their kittens exploring. Some of them hide behind plants while others climb trees.

Leah

Lily

Party time

It's Ellie's birthday and Lily has just arrived at her party. The kittens are excited by the wrapping paper and the decorations, but it's not safe for them to play with the balloons in case they chew on them.

Ellie

21

Mila

22

Chloe

Keeping clean

All kittens learn to lick their fur to keep themselves
clean, but the dolls often help by brushing them
gently so that their fur is free from tangles.

Sleepy kittens

Shhh! Don't wake the little kittens. They are fast asleep after an exciting day playing, exploring, climbing and jumping.

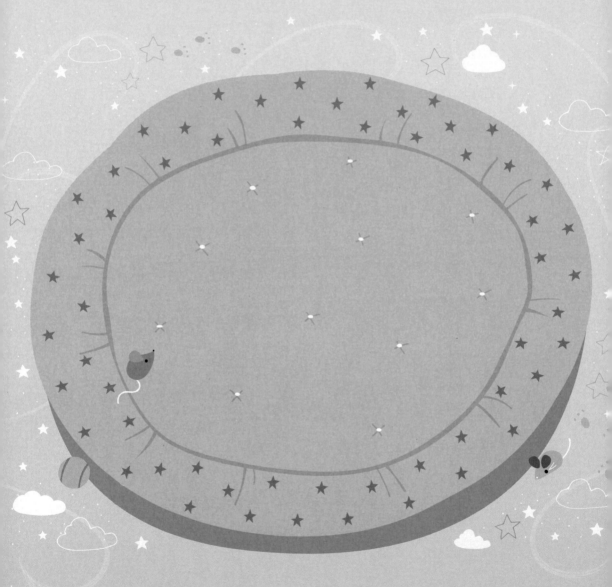

First published in 2021 by Usborne Publishing Limited, 83-85 Saffron Hill, London EC1N 8RT, United Kingdom. usborne.com
Copyright © 2021 Usborne Publishing Limited. The name Usborne and the Balloon logo are registered trade marks of Usborne Publishing Limited. All rights reserved. No part of this publication may be reproduced, stored in a retrieval system or transmitted in any form or by any means without prior permission of the publisher.
First published in America 2021. This edition published 2023. UE

A new kitten
Pages 2-3

A bow for
Izzy's hair

Izzy's
outfit

Nina's
outfit

Visiting the vet
Pages 4-5

Robyn's uniform

Lauren's clothes

In the garden

Millie's outfit

Emily's clothes

Millie's boots

Put Emily's clothes on before her boots.

More stickers for In the garden
Pages 6-7

Cat café
Pages 8-9

Catching leaves
Pages 10-11

Freya's earmuffs and coat

Freya's boots

Lara's holding bunches of leaves.

Lara's outfit

Feeding time
Pages 12-13

Lola's T-shirt

Lola's tray
and apron

Maddie's
outfit

A play date
Pages 14-15

Jessie's top and skirt

Mia's top

Pet store
Pages 16-17

Orla's outfit

Emma's apron

More stickers for the Pet store
Pages 16-17

Exploring outside
Pages 18-19

A flower for
Cassie's hair

Cassie's top and
skirt

Flowers for
Leah's hair

Leah's
outfit

Party time

Lily's skirt

Ellie's top
and skirt

Keeping clean
Pages 22-23

Mila's outfit

Sleepy kittens
Page 24